THE MASTER DREAM: A SHORT GUIDE

KANISHKA SHIVARAM

This book is dedicated to you, the reader.

Contents

Acknowledgements

I would first like to begin by thanking God, the omnipresent for giving me the courage and confidence to pursue this degree and the opportunity to write this book.

Secondly, my utmost thanks is due to my family - my parents: mom - Priyadarshini & dad - Shivaram for supporting me with finances (due to which I didn't take any study abroad loans) and their unconditional moral and emotional support always. Secondly, my sweet younger brother - Kaielash, for being a great companion and support throughout my admissions process. Thirdly, my grandmother - for all her blessings and prayers for me.

Next, I'd like to thank all my institutions that moulded me for being a good candidate for my dream B-school:

"Enlighten. Lead. Change"

"Tamso Maa Jyotirgamaya(Lead us from darkness into light)"

"Love & Serve"

These are the grand mottos of my school - Cluny, undergraduate college - SRCC, and B-school - ESSEC and I endeavor each day to live up to these grand mottos in my personal and professional lives.

My utmost thanks also go to Tamana Suresh Mulchand for giving me the internship which was a mandatory component of the course. While working closely with her, I've always looked up to her during my internship days.

Further, I'd like to express my sincere thanks to my aunt - Vidya Mohan, and uncle - Murali Mohan for their moral support in Singapore while I was living away from home. My deepest thanks also go to my best friend - KP (Krishna Priya) for being an amazing buddy during the completion of my Master's.

Last but not least, my thanks go to all my well-wishers, friends, family, and dear ones that I've missed to include above. I sincerely acknowledge your good intentions towards me and thank you for keeping me always in your prayers.

Foreword

An abroad master's degree is more than a line on your resume. It represents the will, commitment, sacrifice, perseverance, ambition, and quench to succeed despite all odds. It leads you to become a valuable, educated, aware, and virtuous global citizen. However, the journey to getting into your master's degree is not all roses. There are several roadblocks and if you are well aware of them ahead of time, you'll cross the ocean with grace and reach the harbor - your dream school. That is my end goal for you as a reader through this book.

Through this short guide, I aim to make you self-reliant and self-contained in your master's application process. This book is meant for students, young professionals or anyone aspiring to do a master's overseas. I have looked beyond the GRE/GMAT tests and the interview preparation as I'm confident that there are adequate resources in the market for tests and interviews. I have elaborated on the mental makeup and the practical steps required to help you get clarity and guide you through this application journey. Moreover, the interview is just an attempt to understand you personally and ensure you really have the burning desire to pursue that degree. I'm confident that if you have read my book, you'll become self-sufficient to adequately ace the interview round as well.

Besides, I want you to save money from going to expensive consultants in the market and therefore, my attempt is to make you more confident in your own set of skills and help you reach that dream school.

All the Best!!

P.S: For any additional queries on study abroad or if you want to suggest improvements to the book or just understand my journey, feel free to connect with me on LinkedIn or just drop an email at kanishkashivaram@icloud.com

ONE

HOPEFUL NIGHTS

Some do a Master's to earn a degree. Some do it for networking. Some to elevate their career/professional status. Some to expand their knowledge in an area of specialization and some because they are lifelong learners. You may now think you are a mix of the above but my goal when you finish this book is to help you navigate yourself through your chaos and tune into the real you identifying that untapped reason of why you are actually pursuing this master. This is the secret sauce that will run deep while you craft those essays, decide on the college, reach out for LORs and navigate the maze. Whoever you may be, if you have atleast 5% interest in earning a master's degree abroad, this book is for you.

In navigating my puzzle, I went through countless nights thinking of the course, country, college; countless hours wrecking those online resouces and thinking hard if I need to take the help of any professional service. Just to clarify here, I didn't use any professional service for any part of my journey and I solely applied through my own individual efforts. Years of planning and yearning to do a masters abroad finally culminated into the dream of ESSEC

Singapore. The bigger dream of becoming the student ambassador of ESSEC also became a reality and that was my motivation to author this short hand guide as well.

But hey, shall we rewind my journey and talk about the HOW, WHAT AND WHY of it?

I strongly believe, "The only person you need to be accountable in this journey is You".

It maybe relevant here to understand a bit about my background. I basically graduated from SRCC, Delhi University in 2021 in B.com(Hons) (Huge shout out to Prof. Gazala Fareedi who was my biggest inspiration) and wanted to do UPSC(more about it in this chapter). Later, I worked for almost a year as a political consultant and then moved to Singapore for my Masters in Marketing Management and Digital from ESSEC Singapore. During my masters, I also interned with two other leading offices in Singapore.

Now, I'm going to narrate a personal short story which is going to be inspirational for people looking to shift careers through their masters or are just confused about career paths. But if you are none of the two above, feel free to jump forward to the next chapter. So, story time! I've always wanted to become a civil Services Officer and serve India to the best of my capabilities. My passion for it was running high ever since my childhood. I would read all the books written by Dr.APJ Abdul Kalam as he was, is and will always be one of my biggest inspirations after my mother. Inspired by his books, I even wrote a short essay for my country in my earliest school days. Here is a copy of it!: (You'll enjoy if you are a lover of your country)

Oh India! My India!

Oh India! My India! Where do I start and how should I stop admiring you? You are the cradle of human race, the birthplace of human speech, the mother of history, the grandmother of legend and the great grandmother of tradition.

Our most valuable and most artistic materials in the history of man are treasured up in India only. , a pure, young and rich country was born from the blood, sweat and tears of thousands of freedom fighters when J.Nehru, on Aug 15,1947, at the stroke of midnight hour delivered, "The Tryst with Destiny" speech when the whole world slept but India awoke to life, freedom, glory, wisdom, pride and can today boisterously boast of being the world's largest democracy and the fifth largest growing economy with a vibrant media, active civil society, respected judiciary and 'unity in not just diversity but also adversity'. I love, admire and take pride of the fact that the soul of our Indian nation was made with the ambition of greatest men and women who wanted to wipe every tear from every eye and wanted every Indian to labour and work hard to constitute India as a sovereign, socialist, secular and a democratic Republic. The underlying shakti and genius of India lies in the fact that whether he is a Hindu, Muslim, Christian or Sikh, every man will find a common ground under the shelter of Mother India's hospitality. I cannot help being exhilarated looking at the glory of ancient Indian literature, a treasure trove of knowledge, wisdom and heritage from ancient India. From kings to kingdoms, town planning to artistry, scholars to astronomers, philosophers to astrologers, gurus to sishyas, warriors to strong women characters, the list of India's rich past goes on and on,all reflecting the ideal-Vasudhaiva Kutumbakam(The world is one family) enshrined in Rig Veda.

Nations are built by the imagination of untiring, enthusiastic effort of generations. One generation transfers the fruits of it to another which then takes forward the mission. As the coming generation also has its dreams and aspirations for the nation's future, therefore adding something from its side to the national vision; which the next generation strives hard to achieve. This process goes on and the nation climbs the steps of glory and gains higher strengths. A nation without a vision is like a ship cruising on the high seas without any aim or direction. It's the clarity of the national vision that constantly drives people towards the goal. Reflecting on the glorious past of India, let us all collectively set THE GREAT INDIAN DREAM- where every citizen would work hard, prosper and succeed through innovation and hard work and once successful, every citizen would give back to the society that made him/her what he/she is.

This Independence day, let us all collectively vow to cherish and follow the noble ideals that inspired our national struggle for freedom and uphold and protect the sovereignty, unity and integrity of India, to ensure 'SATYAMEVA JAYATE'-Truth alone triumphs. There is just one country, one India which we all want to become a better place. We all want a nation that is rich and respected in the world. We all want a society with good values. Thank you for reading my Great Indian Dream and I hope, from now on, you will make it yours too.

Irony, I left India for my dream of doing a master's abroad. I agree if you may think that it's wise to pursue your long-held passion but I wouldn't agree more if you say it is far more sensible to switch gears. The right action at the right time in the right age gives the right result. Any right gone wrong in the above equation may collapse the whole spectrum.

I have toiled immensely for this exam since 8th grade however, decided that I would give only one attempt in this exam. If I didn't make it in that attempt, I was sure of what my Plan B was - Master. Well, you should now, probably realize that not all Plan As are the best, and not all Plan Bs are better. Sometimes, Plan B can turn out to be a better fit for you than your Plan A. Remember, by choosing to have so many plans, you are not choosing to **fail** your Plan A but instead, you are choosing to **win** despite any odds. Therefore, this short personal example above is to inspire you to forge ahead and go for your MASTER DREAM immaterial of the setbacks, failures, or unsatisfied career paths you may have gone through because in the end, it was all worth it and if it weren't for my masters, I wouldn't have written this book today.

Sure, the transition is not easy but trust me, it's worth it. Convert your pain into purpose and a source of inspiration urging you to chase that higher education overseas.

"Let craft, ambition, spite
Be quenched in Reason's night,
Till weakness turn to might,
Till what is dark be light,
Till what is wrong be right".
"Prepare for all your days and meet them ever alike;
When you are the anvil - bear;
When you are the hammer - strike".

TWO

THE APPLICATION DECISION

Plan A. Plan B. Plan C. Plan D. My brain was filled with these plans and figuring them out during the inital sprint. Let's break it down - what are these plans? and what do I advise you to do so that your confusion turns into a decision? Well, that's the goal of this chapter.

My plan A was to do a Masters in Marketing Management and Digital (MMD) from ESSEC Asia-Pacific. However, given the high competitiveness and rigorous selection rates, I had multiple other plans. Plan B was another reputable uni in London. Plan C was a well-known uni in the UK. Plan D was a great B-school in Paris and so on. I had it decoded till Plan J. To remind you, by planning so much it isn't that we are expecting Plan A to fail rather we are preparing to win despite all the odds.

TIP: Choose your Plans wisely. Make an informed decision.

So, to do this clearly, I suggest you prepare an Excel with columns of the following:

1. School Name
2. QS Ranking Assessment

3. Course Structure Assessment
4. Country Assessment
5. Affordability Assessment
6. Alumni Assessment
7. Post-study opportunities and visa assessment
8. Deadlines

Now, before we jump and decode each one of these, here are some general guidelines. In each of the above columns, just indicate with ✓ or **X.** Do not assess on a points basis as that will only add more confusion to the chaos. Step 0 would be to decide on all the courses you are keen on pursuing. Think over it, ask your closest circle, and make a wise decision. Alternatively, if you have two or three courses in mind (Eg. Masters in Marketing, Masters in Finance, etc..), you can prepare as many individual Excels (one Excel for one course) as you want. For all of these excels you can apply the same generic principles I'm going to elaborate on in this chapter.

- QS Rankings: This is probably one of the factors that influenced my decision to apply, as I see these rankings as not mere scorecards but a holistic approach to analyzing a Uni/B-school from diverse angles. I personally prefer the QS Rankings as I aligned with the parameters of their rankings the best. Primarily, to assess if a particular institution would be a good fit for me, I'd generally restrict it to the top 20-25 of the QS Rankings for that subject. Secondarily, I would also look at the overall Business school or university rankings and compare them with other rankings such as Financial Times, etc.
- Course Structure Assessment: The next step is to look at the course modules on the official college website and

assess if that's something you would actually be interested in pursuing. For example, when I was skimming through course modules of various B-schools for my Masters in Marketing, I landed upon course modules that were highly analytical and decided that wouldn't be my cup of tea. Rather, ESSEC had a perfect mix of analytical, theoretical, and practical knowledge which made it the first choice for me. Therefore, look at the course structure and assess if it truly sparks your curiosity and interest in you. If yes, then this gets a tick, if not, you know the answer.

- Country Assessment: While choosing a country, I would like to highlight all the key and valid factors that need to be considered here. As you would be away from home with a time difference, this consideration shouldn't be undervalued. I was lucky to have my close aunt and uncle here in Singapore and I thank them immensely for their invaluable emotional and moral support throughout my masters. I can't help but quote these beautiful lines which say that a plant doesn't just bloom out of the blue, how well a plant blooms is directly proportional to the environment in which it blooms. Well, that environment here is the country for you. The other components while assessing the country should be weather conditions (if your body would be adaptable to it), food and accommodation options, post-study visa options when you are still looking for a job, quality of public transportation, and finally most importantly, crime rates and safety! Of course, a country may not be able to tick all of these factors above but if most of the crucial ones are covered, then this column gets a tick as well!

- Affordability Assessment: Many times I get queries regarding affordability. Questions such as: Is it a good idea to take a loan? Will the course be worth it? Will I be able to pay back in time? and similar ones. Well, let me try my best to answer them here. Taking a study-abroad loan can be a great investment in your future, but it's essential to carefully evaluate your family's personal situation before making a decision. Understand the loan's interest rate, repayment tenure, and monthly installments. Education loans often come with flexible repayment options but ensure they are manageable within your expected graduation giving adequate room of allowance for time to land a job (around 3-6 months)

Pro-Tips to minimize financial risks:

- Scholarships & Grants: Apply to as many scholarships and grants as possible to reduce your loan amount.

- Part-time work: Check if your student visa and your desired university allow you to work part-time as this will greatly help to offset living costs while studying. These part-time work can be internships in your field of study or any other work that picks your interest in which you can create a win-win by positively contributing to society and getting paid back in return.

- Loan moratorium period: Many student loans offer a grace period before repayment begins giving you time to secure a job.

Lastly, if you think you are confident in your plan based on realistic salary expectations and landing a job in the market, go for loans. If not, try to avoid them.

Post this brief analysis, if you feel the tuition + living costs of that country are affordable for you, give that uni a tick for affordability. If not, just an X.

- Alumni Assessment: LinkedIn is a powerhouse for this assessment. Connect with as many alumni as possible and gather as many diverse perspectives as you possibly can. If possible, based on the availability of the person, try scheduling a short call with him/her.

Tip: Reach out to Student Ambassadors

The responsiveness of alumni will become a big red/green flag as their responsiveness will not just help understand their experience but also post-admission for career tips and advice and course navigation advice. If they are responsive, these are the topics you need to ask them (feel free to frame questions around these topics):

1. Their experience and review of the course and school
2. Their take on the country-weather-food-accommodation options
3. Part-time work/internship opportunities
4. Post-study opportunities
5. Quality of teachers and resource availability
6. Diversity of class profile
7. Networking opportunities
8. Career centre feedback

The above is not exhaustive; you can ask all these & more during the call. Do not ask all the above questions in a single message. Keep the first question short, crisp, powerful, and simple. Then slowly ask one by one. Focus on building a good rapport with the person as it is another avenue for networking and you never know when who can come to help.

- Post-study opportunities assessment: To assess this, look at where the alumni are placed. Then look at their general profiles - background and past experiences. This will give you an idea of the kind of profile that uni or b-school accepts. Typically, 0-2 years of work experience before a master's is a good number. Look at the companies the alumni are working in and think if you'd like to work for them. For example, in my case, some ESSEC MMD Alumni were working in big luxury firms, which aligned with my aspirations. Likewise, make an assessment and accordingly give this a ✓ or X.

**"When you turn your confusion into a decision based on solid assessment,
chaos moulds into confidence, and that is the secret power you need to ace that admissions interview."**

THREE

DECODING THE "WHAT" & "HOW"

By now, I would assume that you would have the winning Excel sheet ready. So why wait? Let's dive into the "What" and "How"!

A famous man once said that one can never be a good human being if he/she doesn't have an idea of "What is good". Similarly, one can never be great at Master if he/she doesn't have a clear idea of what he/she is getting into. From my experience, Master is not about going back to books (in fact my course had very limited books to be referred to), instead there is a focus on case studies, theoretical understanding, and hands-on projects conquering practical knowledge.

Therefore, I recommend you to go through the course website & understand all the key requirements. Decode a list of specific qualities that they are looking for in their ideal student as it varies from uni to uni/b-school to B-school. Next, understand the admissions process, and the timeline & reach out to the ambassadors. The application process is the bridge between your dream and its realization. It is both, an art and science requiring sustained motivation, organization & above all understanding what is that "one thing" each institution is looking for. To break it down,

1. Understanding the key requirements: This component, as I said earlier, highly varies from course to course & institution to institution. Typically, transcripts of previous degree, GMAT/GRE test scores (depending on the course), LORs, Application Essays, and a CV/Resume.

2. Crafting a well-structured timeline: Start with the same Excel we used before. Use that as a base and create a timeline for the upcoming month balancing your other priorities. Give sufficient allowance for professors/colleagues to write LORs for you. A good idea at this stage would be to start with shortlisting professors managers or senior leaders you'd like to approach for LORs and let them know that you would need their letters.

A Sample timeline: (Remember, the studying abroad journey is not a sprint, it's a marathon!)

- 1 August = Shortlist people to approach for LORs

- 2 August = Drafting Essay 1 for XYZ Bschool + reaching out to people for LORs

- 3 August = Completing Essay 1 for XYZ Bschool + Drafting Essay 2 for YXZ Uni

- 4 August = Follow-ups on LORs

GOES ON

- 26 August = Call with Mr. AMB from XYZ Bschool (This is when you are fully done with all the essays for XYZ Bschool)

So the above is a sample timeline. You can create your own timeline based on deadlines and this would allow you to work backward allocating sufficient time for drafting compelling essays, preparing for tests, and securing recommendations.

Note: I haven't emphasized preparation for the GRE/ GMAT in this timeline or the book as I'm confident that there are ample resources available in the market for the same.

TIP: Submit early, and apply in the early rounds of admission - Preferably R1 or R2 to maximize your chance of securing the seat and also scholarships.

3. Seeking feedback: No wise human would ever ignore constructive feedback. Constructive feedback builds a person and adds immense value to the journey. As the saying goes 'A stitch in time saves nine', similarly, good feedback taken positively at the right time secures your admission. So, this is the time to reach out to your mentors, trusted friends or family members, and seniors and seek feedback on the things you've worked on. A word of caution here: too much feedback can lead you to confusion as well. Filter them out and take the part that truly adds value to this journey of yours.

Opportunity
They do me wrong who say I come no more
When once I knock and fail to find you in;
For every day I stand outside your door,
And bid you wake, and rise to fight and win.

Wail not for precious chances passed away,
Weep not for golden ages on the wane!
Each night I burn the records of the day-
At sunrise every soul is born again!

Laugh like a boy at splendors that have sped,
To vanished joys be blind and deaf and dumb;
My judgements seal the dead past with its dead,
But never bind a moment yet to come.

Though deep in mire, wring not your hands and weep;
I lend my arm to all who say "I Can!"
No shame-faced outcast ever sank so deep,
But yet might rise and be again a man.

Dost thou behold thy lost youth all aghast?
Dost reel from righteous Retribution's blow?
Then turn from blotted archives of the past,
And find the future's pages white as snow.

Art thou a mourner? Rouse thee from thy spell;
Art thou a sinner? Sins may be forgiven;
Each morning gives thee wings to flee from hell,
Each night a star to guide thy feet to heaven.

- Walter Malone

FOUR

THE WHY: IS IT YOUR SOUL'S CALLING?

Pursuing a Master's degree isn't just a commitment for one or few years, it is a lifelong decision as it will shape your career path. It is a monumental decision often involving significant financial, personal, and professional investments, Understanding your "Why" will not just make you build your unique purpose for SOPs/Essays to stand out but also will internally motivate you to make the right choice. The various reasons that I can possibly think of are elaborated below:

1. Career advancement: In today's competitive job market, a bachelor's degree is no longer the golden ticket it once was. A master's degree will set you apart, signaling expertise and a commitment to lifelong learning. It often acts as a stepping stone to:

- Leadership roles: Many managerial and executive positions require a postgraduate degree as a baseline in their qualification requirements.
- Specialized fields: For professions like data science, AI, Luxury brand management, political marketing, etc., advanced knowledge equips you with the right expertise.
- Industry Shift: If you are looking to pivot into a new industry (as I elaborated in my first chapter), a master's degree equips you with the tools to make that transition seamless.

2. Global exposure: Studying abroad means living abroad, working abroad, making new friends globally, thinking globally, becoming more culturally sensitive, and developing all the values required for being a good global citizen. Living abroad teaches you to become more independent (both financially & emotionally), resilient, culturally sensitive, and a 100 other values that money can't buy.

3. Access to expertise & resources: A master's program connects you with a wealth of resources that can transform your academic and professional journey. Some of them are:

√ World-class faculty

√ Advanced libraries, labs, research centers

√ Exclusive opportunities with partner firms and top companies giving you the golden ticket to internships, mentorships & job placements.

4. A sense of accomplishment: Earning a master's degree is more than a line on your resume - it's a personal milestone. It represents three key things:

√ Perseverance: The dedication to see the journey through, from application to graduation

√Ambition: A commitment to improving yourself and chasing your dreams, no matter the hurdles

√A lifelong credential: A degree from a prestigious institution is a badge of honor that carries weight for the rest of your life.

5. Impact beyond yourself:

'A child always asks - "What can you do for me?" whereas a leader asks "What can I do for you?" '

Similarly, the master's degree you pursue will have the following impact on society:

- Breaking gender stereotypes: This applies to you if you are a woman and especially the first in your family to go overseas and pursue a degree
- Inspiring others: Your journey can motivate your peers, family, or mentees to dream big and aim higher. As Carla Harris says, "True leaders make leaders". Be a true leader.
- Giving back: With your newfound knowledge and skills, you can make a difference in your community or industry, creating a ripple effect of positive change.
- Expanding opportunities: As you grow, you create space for others to grow alongside - whether through mentorship, innovation, collaboration, or even simply - just by pursuing your journey joyously.

Therefore, the WHY behind pursuing a master's degree is deeply personal but its impact is universal. Whether it's about climbing the corporate ladder, building lifelong skills or simply following your passion - the decision to enroll in a master's program abroad is a powerful intent: the intent to grow, excel & make a difference. Understanding your motivations not only helps you commit to the journey but also ensures that every step you take is purposeful and fulfilling.

Why did I choose ESSEC and why MMD? Short answer, all the good reasons above. The long answer, it's ranked no. 2 worldwide as per QS Rankings, triple crown accreditations, a perfect blend of theory and practical exposure, international study trip, diversity of cohort, Singapore - Asia Pacific location, Digital Marketing Challenge component, mandatory credit-bearing internship, strong partnerships with leading brands and corporate firms and many such similar ones.

"The appearance of things changes according to the emotions and thus we see the magic and beauty in them, while the magic & beauty are really in ourselves."

- The Broken Wings, Khalil Gibran

FIVE

CRAFTING A WINNING ESSAY

TIP 1: Don't use AI. While it may be tempting, it will be the single deadliest weapon in your application that will instantly rule you out!

TIP 2: Do not copy-paste someone else's SOP/Essay.

TIP 3: Do not go by the standard format that consultants in the market may advise you. While this is not a clear no, it is better to have your uniqueness in the essay from A to Z.

The essay is your voice, your story, your Unique Selling proposition, and your chance to stand out. Admissions committees read hundreds - if not thousands of applications. Don't aim to draft the perfect essay in one go. Initially, just write whatever comes to your mind. Think over it, take a day's time, re-read it & revise it. This is how you deliver your excellent essay - repeated revisions.

"Aim for excellence, not perfection"

A good essay will surely win the heart of the admissions committee and tip the scales in your favor showcasing who you are, why you belong & what you can bring to the program. In this chapter, we'll explore how to write an essay that not only grabs attention but leaves a lasting impression. In this chapter, we'll explore how to write an essay that not only grabs attention but leaves a lasting impression.

1. Understand the Purpose

Before you begin writing, it's crucial to understand what admissions committees are looking for. Your essay is not just about listing achievements; it's about answering three key questions:

Who are you? Highlight your personality, experiences, and values.

Why this program? Show how the program aligns with your goals.

What value will you bring? Emphasize your unique perspective and potential contributions to the cohort.

2. Tell Your Story

Your essay is your personal narrative—a story that reflects your journey, aspirations, and why you're ready for this next step.

Start with a Hook: Open with an anecdote, a challenge you overcame, or a moment of clarity that sparked your decision to pursue this degree.

Example: "I still remember the moment I held my first marketing campaign proposal in my hands—it was a realization of my passion for connecting ideas with people."

Connect the Dots: Link your past experiences, current aspirations, and future goals in a coherent and compelling way.

Be Authentic: Avoid clichés or trying to fit into what you think the committee wants. Let your genuine voice shine through.

3. Align with the Program

Admissions committees want to see that you've done your homework and understand how their program fits into your plans.

Mention Specifics: Highlight courses, professors, or initiatives that attract you to the program.

Example: "The opportunity to learn from Professor Smith's groundbreaking research on digital consumer behavior excites me, as it directly aligns with my career goal of leading digital transformation in the retail sector."

Explain the Fit: Describe how the program's strengths align with your needs and how it will help you grow.

4. Showcase Your Value

This is your chance to highlight what makes you unique and how you'll contribute to the program's diversity and culture.

Emphasize Your Strengths: Whether it's your leadership skills, international experience, or creative problem-solving, tie these traits back to how they'll benefit the program.

Example: "Having worked in multicultural teams across three continents, I bring a global perspective that will enrich class discussions on cross-border strategies."

Be Future-Focused: Discuss how the program will empower you to make an impact, whether in your field, community or beyond.

5. Nail the Structure

A clear and logical structure ensures your essay flows smoothly and keeps the reader engaged.

Introduction: Start with a strong opening that captures attention and sets the tone.

Body Paragraphs: Divide the essay into sections that address your background, motivation, and fit for the program. Use transitions to maintain coherence.

Conclusion: End with a powerful closing statement that ties everything together and leaves a lasting impression.

Example: "This program isn't just the next step in my career—it's the key to unlocking my full potential and contributing meaningfully to the global marketing landscape."

6. Avoid Common Pitfalls

X Generic Statements: Avoid vague phrases like "I want to make a difference" without explaining how.

X Overemphasis on Achievements: While accomplishments are important, focus on what you learned from them and how they shape your future goals.

X Neglecting Proofreading: Typos and grammatical errors can undermine an otherwise strong essay. Always proofread multiple times or seek feedback.

7. Practical Tips for Success

Start Early: Give yourself enough time to brainstorm, write, and revise.

Seek Feedback: Share your draft with trusted mentors or peers for constructive criticism.

Keep it Concise: Stick to the word limit and ensure every sentence adds value.

Be Confident: Don't undersell yourself—this is your time to shine.

Crafting a winning essay is about more than ticking boxes; it's about showcasing your authenticity, vision, and determination. Think of it as a conversation with the admissions committee—a chance to connect with them on a personal level and show why you're the perfect fit.

A great essay doesn't just secure your spot in the program; it becomes the first chapter in your journey toward achieving ***The Master Dream***. Let your passion and potential drive your words, and watch as your story inspires the decision-makers to choose you.

> **"Think ever of rising higher.**
> **Let it be your only thought.**
> **Even if your object be not attained,**
> **the thought itself will have raised you."**
>
> **- Thirukural**

Sample Winning Essays

ESSAY 1
Why do you want to pursue this career path? (250 words or less)

When I was a child, I hoped that I would have superpowers one day. I thought that I would become a billionaire by selling products across the world through a magic carpet. That was my idea of making a difference in the world. Now that I have grown up and find myself having to make important career decisions, I realize that this magic carpet is the (xyz) and the tool is (abc). With a more realistic perception of life, I believe that (xyz) is truly an effective way to make a difference in our business world and I aspire to become a (XYZ) Manager.

There are several reasons I chose this career path. First of all, I am very passionate about (ABC) and aspire to leave a footprint in the marketing industry by profoundly impacting the way (abc) is done in the world. I am keen on pursuing this career path as I know that this is exactly where my true calling is. Associating myself with multiple organizations in this domain, I aim to accelerate it further by broadening my scope of vision and acquiring rich professional expertise in this field.

Additionally, my interest in (abc) will help me take pleasure in advancing my career in (xyz) which has (abc) at the helm of its activities. My ambitious nature would also

reflect in my (abc) strategies and enable the target audience to set a high benchmark of
themselves.

I envision specializing in the field of (xyz) through this course and securing the position of
(xyz) Manager at a prominent company in (Target country) or pan-world. In this capacity, I
specifically yearn to formulate and execute ground-breaking (abc) strategies that will shake the
world of (xyz). My prime goal is to associate myself with a company that has its reach across
horizons. Few years down the line, I aim to climb up the ladder and be in the top positions of the firm
where I would be leading the company holistically.

However, not limiting myself to practicing (abc), I also desire to contribute to the theory and stack
of (xyz). I have grown up admiring (Mr. ABC - a prominent author in the industry) and have read his books and ideas on how to win,
influence, and dominate the (abc) world. I would combine my learning with my gained professional
experience to propose theories on modern (abc) that would help future generations.

ᐅᐅᐅ

ESSAY 2

How does this school and course align with you on a personal and professional level? (250 words or less)

Ancient Indian philosophers have divided human life into three main parts: body, soul and mind. This
can be equated to personal, spiritual and professional

dimension of one's life. My deep interest in philosophy had led me to questioning the meaning of human existence and engaging with mature philosophies of the world from a young age. Examples include Indian masterpiece Bhagvad Gita, Greek thoughts of Plato, Marcus Aurelius, books on The Man's search for meaning and many more.

At a personal level, my teachers have significantly influenced and shaped the person I am today. I admire each one of them and as they entered the class, I used to see radiation of knowledge from them. To quote a specific instance, during my 8 th grade English classes, my teacher had introduced me to the life of Dr. Abdul Kalam and from that very moment till now, I have been deeply admiring him and following his footsteps. I started reading multiple books of Dr. Kalam and even read all those books that influenced his way of thinking. I admire him for the moral standards and values he upholds and at a personal level, my moral ethical code and integrity matters more than anything else to me.

At a spiritual level, I have a deep curiosity to understand the core of every religion and my schooling at a Convent and upbringing in a Hindu family has added to my diverse perspective. All along, I have managed to maintain the principles of ethics and integrity which my Christians run Convent school instilled in me. I have read multiple books authored by Swami Vivekananda, The Holy Bible, The Holy Bhagvad Gita, Ikigai and numerous others. All these have made me realize that the ultimate goal of human life is happiness and that the only place to find it is within each one of us.

At a professional level, I understand that on an average, almost 40% of our time is spent on the career
path we have chosen. Besides financial rewards, work gives me the opportunity to refine and share
knowledge, build relationships, help people, overcome personal challenges, grow as a professional, and
participate in a social environment. Being able to create large scale impact and leave a footprint in the
sands of time is what makes me a good human being and I yearn to make this a life of purpose through
my professional dimension.

Sample Resume Format

PS: Please excuse if there is an error in displaying the right format due to page size and printing issues. You can drop me an email (address given in Foreword), and I shall mail you the winning resume format.

YOUR NAME Mobile: +91 88888888

xyz@gmail.com

ACADEMIC QUALIFICATIONS

Bachelor of (XYX) (College Name) (Grade) 2018-2021

12th grade (School name) 98.5% 2018

10th grade (School name) 98.8% 2016

ACADEMIC ACHIEVEMENTS (List all academic achievements - Sample list here)

- District 1st and State 3rd rank in 10th board examinations; District 1st and State 2nd rank in 12th board examinations
- XYZZZZ

PROFESSIONAL EXPERIENCE

(Title of position)

intern

(Company Name) (June'22 - Oct'22)

- Certified "No.1 Best ABC Intern" among more than 300 interns nationally
- Created innovative marketing strategies to increase brand awareness about '(Company Name)'
- Designed and edited xyz tools and zbc instruments; boosted volunteers rate by 50%
- Planned and implemented xyz to increase digital media success rate by over 75%
- Led a team of 15+ interns and delivered record team

results, improving digital media
visibility by 3X

(Title of Position)
(Company Name)
(June'21 - Sep'21)

• Among 5 out of 600+ interns selected to work with Core team on abc strategy
• Increased online traffic by 40% through SEO, link building and content marketing
• Planned and implemented measures to optimize sales funnel, increase MoM revenue by 25%
• Designed in lead generation strategies resulting in profits of INR 500000

(Title of Position)
(Company Name)
(Aug'22 - Present)

• Devised leading campaign idea "(Campaign name)" for nation's leading and world' top xyz
• Devised numerous campaign and political strategies for xyz increasing support base by 4X
• End-to-end campaign management from ideation to execution impacting 10,00,000 people
• Handled 20+ senior most abc field's clients boosting their brand among public by over 10X
• Led a team of over 30 campaign analysts boosting their brand marketing by 80%
• Liaised with stakeholders between key abc office bearers for Social Media Analytics and Marketing Management of key (field) trends Pan-India

POSITIONS OF RESPONSIBILITY

President
ABC Club

(2019-2020)
- Led a team of 40+ members to handle parallel execution of 10+ events at ABC-One of Asia's
largest student festivals with a footfall of 1 Lakh+ students
- Raised sponsorship worth INR1,00,000+ through marketing strategies
- Increased brand awareness of society by over 10X through SEO, link building and content marketing

President
XYZ Club
(2019-2020)
- Pioneered ABC event which made its entry into World Records for being a novel (abc) run by students
- Supervised a team of 80+ members towards execution of (ABC)
- Organized 10+ pan-India competitions throughout the year

Vice-President
AXZ Club
(2019-2020)
- Spearheaded the ideation and execution of XYZ's MUN increasing YoY participation by 30%
- Conducted several on-campus debate leagues nationally with a footfall of 50K+ students
- Contributed several top-notch research articles on latest political and international affairs whichincreased engagement ratio by 80%

House Captain
School Name
(2017-2018)

- Led the entire school team of 3500+ students towards winning the year end Championship Trophy
- Pioneered "Project xyz" towards free girls' tuition classes in school for nearby slums

House Vice-Captain
School Name
(2016-17)

- Assisted the Captain towards winning the prestigious "March-Past Trophy"
- Led a cohort of 1500+ students towards various sports, academic and other events
- Pioneered various strategies to instill discipline and punctuality among students much recognised by the school head

EXTRACURRICULARS AND ACCOMPLISHMENTS
INTERNATIONAL
- (List of all international accomplishments)

PUBLICATIONS
- (List of all your publications or research pieces)

TITLES
- (If you hold, any outstanding titles in extra-curriculars, list them down here)

OTHERS
- (Other significant accomplishments)

ᗞᗞᗞ